CHAMBERS of the HEART

RAGE/coraje

LOVE/amor

REVOLUTION/revolución

EVOLUTION/evolución

RAGE
coraje

Chamber I

Revolución

Dreamt about the heavens
falling into my life
tainted by the blood of my brothers
crying out for me

Angry mob of society
disillusioned by their own expectations of life
exploited somehow and feeling cheated
because the violence wasn't enough to feed their ego

Dreamt about my ancestors shouting
into my veins about the bruises on their souls
left behind by the assholes in control

Rusted words of peace
promises filled with lies saying
without pain there is no surfacing

Dreamt about mi tierra Aztlán
mi raza mestiza
twist of fate left us
on the wrong side of the tracks
fire burning within

Wake up from the dream you were fed as a child
by the same government who's keeping you down
expected to remain exiled in "freedom"
silence is not your weapon

El sol consumiendo, sacrificed identity?
let me tell you something
justice is never served to the seeker
and my dreams escape me

Wake Up

Who's throwing the dice
keeping the score
talk of evolution
contemplate redemption
of the human
here comes a Revolution

Strike against strike
they're imposing the lies
feeding us rights
that weren't chosen
there's no drifting from cries
as they terrorize, create borders

Decide to activize
thus realize the motion
to recognize & devise a plan
to expand the fight for our land

Demand liberty
not some cages and fees
keeping us down on our knees
won't you wake up and see the disorder

At Night

at night the light blows out
what route have we embarked upon
the dawn stalked the voiceless
made them less
would we regress
to repeat the beat of the war drum
the hymn of peace
does not cease
thus does increase
to form release
growing
sowing
reaping
knowing
that life should not be taken in vain
the stain explodes
the gun reloads
the mind numb soldier kills
behind the clouds of liberty
i'll make you free
fills the heavens with rain
wills the cycle of slaying
a tear the fear
mama hold me near
behold
history unfolds
the sight
the flight
of people sold
for monetary gain
slain without mercy
by democracy
we will save your soil
but not your souls
your blood spilled for oil

the veil recoils
the hypocrisy
of this U.S.A.

you say
you will protect me
represent this sea
of masses
of different classes, colors, & creeds
instead i reject
that which you claim to be
massacring fellow beings
in my name
its this government i blame
it's you i shame
open your eyes
we are the same
under the rising sun
a day will come
america will weep
those numbed in sleep
will awake and plea
for mother earth to forgive thee
and then love will become one
all that i am
all that we are
all that we were
all that we will be
a light
at night

Deep

An emotion runs deep, steep
slipping to the core or corpses of men
when will it end
are we to mend differences like this
a backstabbing kiss
we bleed
need to connect
reject the lies
the sighs run deep, weep
creeping into unconsciousness
the cries
the reasons why
a child so mild must endure pain
witness rain of bullets and bombs
that lead a family to tombs
the womb is cut
the wound it hurt
i blurt out words to heal my sorrow
will my innocent ones see tomorrow
a sea of death
a breath exhale deep, eternal sleep
the eyes are shut
the man is shot
the woman's mouth distorts a shout
piercing the soul of all that is...

Fight

fight for what you stand for
because if you don't, it's all fake
fight for what you believe & love & live for
because if you don't, they win

fight & take down the sky
with the waters of your tears
fight & move the world
to hear their life exploited throughout the years

if you decide the world
no longer deserves to hear those words
then you can stand
in the midst of your soul & realize you tried

when you fought for that worth gaining
& lost your so called life amongst their minds
just know that what you stood for
was & is & will survive in the echo of your voice

Batalla

Cinco de Mayo
Batalla de Puebla
Also Known As
Drink up
Sink in
Forget Self
Under Sombreros & Imported Beer
I declare this a stolen "holiday"
because the Batalla lives on everyday
The barrio is under siege
by guns, gringos, and greed
This is not my abuela's memory
History distorted as it may be
is not for sale
Don't get me wrong
I love tequila as much as Frida did
but let us remember our Heroes with dignity
Strive to live a piece of that victory
because there are still Batallas to be won
Here & now
All the blood, sweat, and tears
continue year after year &
Life is not a commercial
Batalla de El Sereno,
Lincoln Heights,
Highland Park,
Boyle Heights,
and all the forgotten gente.
Also Known As
Rising up
Tuning in
Remembering Self
Over Códices & Subversive Actions
I declare this a universal movement
because it's time
¡Que viva la Revolución, cabrónes!

sí se puede

you sir took the words from Mi Gente to win your campaign of "HOPE"
YES WE CAN means SI SE PUEDE & if my memory serves me correctly
it was never up for sale...we were never up for sale
you promised immigration reform
you pretended to be of the people for the people
but at night when the lights are out
you strip of ancestral memories
where once we were all the same
no borders, no money, no blame
you promised to bring our soldiers back
you pretended to care for the boys & girls who risk their lives for the red,
white, & blue
but at noon when the sun is hot
you abandon the route to change
where once we were to be free
no war machine, no blood for oil, no greed
you promised things that were not yours to promise
you pretended in all the right places
but at dawn when the light comes up
you will remember a place
where once we were bearers of our own destiny
no wishes, no promises, no "HOPE"
you can keep your change, your "hope", your yes we can
because mi gente is born of struggle, born of cosmic ancestry, born of the
maize
SI SE PUEDE is ours to shout, to claim, to keep
SI SE PUEDE without your corrupt system
SI SE PUEDE without wall street
SI SE PUEDE without your pyramid of lies
SI SE PUEDE is respect to la madre tierra
SI SE PUEDE with the truth
SI SE PUEDE with peace
SI SE PUEDE with love
you, sir, took the words from Mi Gente to sell your campaign of "HOPE"
YES WE CAN means SI SE PUEDE & if my memory serves me correctly
it was never up for sale...we were never up for sale

por siempre

once upon a time
había una vez
in a place not far from here
a binding together of thoughts
like paperbacks
that tell a tale
no holding back
of outrage
that emerges
as you burn me
stamp me
condemn me
take away my cuentos
try to censor the spirit of mi gente
presente
we are here to stay
because the more you ignore me
the closer i get
the louder i get
the stronger i get
linking memories
of our saga
like hardcovers
the first edition
never the last
always a story
to be told
life unfolds
the twisted hair
holding cosmic words
uses breath like ink
that spills forth
truth on paper
the cantos
the versos

the símbolos
that rewrite
the mentiras
the fairytales
the lies that failed
ban me
suppress me
prohibit me
take away my books
try to limit the soul of mi pueblo
rebelde
we will not submit
we will awaken
because our memoirs
both tragic & epic
are authentic & sublime
they will transcend
time, people, & borders
& even if the pages
of our storytellers
are set ablaze
our leyendas will spread
like the fire that consumed them
& flourish in the hearts of our semillas
in flor y canto
por siempre

Opuesto

oppressed
and we're not talking
about legendary i'm your victim
we mean repressed
hidden behind masks
as most human beings are
only because our color
wasn't pure enough
our hands worked & cut
not for our land but yours
for your profit your greed
only because our time
meant your dime
opposition between
the in between
rich poor
you say nothing
we stay silent
so it works that way
division stems
from ignorance

los illuminati

symbols & signs
engraved in our minds
the all seeing eye
keeps you in line
the triangle
keeps you entangled
the owl
keeps you in trance
numbers & places
secret embraces
all around us
subliminal dust
i do not trust
the keepers of time
locked us in a cage
forget your sublime
the keepers of space
seclude us from us
forget your divine
the keepers of matter
enslave us with images
forget you're free
wake up slowly
because it burns
however do it anyway
because it hurts
to stay asleep

Water es Vida

these words will flow
forth like water
for warrior travelers
thirsty for truth
a stream of transparent
molecules that springs
from the mother earth
Agua dulce
Agua ardiente
Agua is Life
cleansing agent
in time of change
feminine energy
transforms wine back
to water
elixir of life

I will not bottle your essence
because that would be like
bottling up my tears
sacred drops
soothing rain
lakes of fire
unconscious stream
as deep as ocean blue
you & I together raza
like waves upon waves
under full moons
bringing up unsettled
sands to surface
nothing less than
currents of Love
rivers of remembrance
wash away scars

he who controls the water
enslaves the world
she who pollutes the water
destroys herself
he who puts a price on the water
steals from his mother's womb
la madre misma
will curse your
flouride fortune &
fountains of filth
because el agua
no se vende
the precious resource
is free &
when contained
will dry up in your mouth
slip thru your hands
& flow back to its
place of origin
like these words
water will flow
free forever
flow forever
flow free

Water es Vida
I take mine
pure & unrefined
you should too

Walking Contradiction

because I am a walking contradiction
I own a Prius when I should really be walking
stop giving money to BIG OIL
I own a Mac when I should really be recycling paper
stop supporting Corporate Companies & killing trees
I listen to world news
when I should be listening to myself
I go to Starbucks before the protest
because I buy your music,
watch your movies,
go to your concerts,
eat at your restaurants
& follow you blindly
while I think I'm free
because I am plugged into your matrix
& I can't break out
because your system is all I've ever known
because I have too many shoes,
too much clothes,
so much stuff that buries me
& I forget why I'm here
because I'm vegetarian
but my favorite boots were leather
because I'm a revolutionary & a radical
but I'm also a mother
& I would not bomb my own children
because of this & more
we are all a walking contradiction

Masochist

is there a part of me
that didn't want this to prevail?

so I get to sink into
that deep dark place
I know so well

so I forget all beauty
stars & rainbows of being

so I go back to the familiar
play victim
hear you console me

I will not wallow
in the depths of this sea

I must remember
search for meaning

I will try
try
try again

do not give up
do not give in

purification thru fire
the martyr

I would lie
if I'm not disappointed

I reclaim
that which is stolen

land identity truth

All you wish
I never knew

city of angels

almost to the top
careful not to fall

fall into the chaos mundane
seeking mesmerized injection
questioning a life of rejection
city of angels gone insane

lost in lustful affection
calling us devils in pain
kids defined by addiction
subdued by tracks in vein

fleeing from falsified dictation
anarchistic discourse of the brain
confused by oppressed affliction
between heaven and hells train

six
six
six
seven
almost to perfection

Nowhere Girl

sadness
long eternal
sadness
eyes not yet old enough to comprehend
behold impurity of men
thoughts too clouded to remind herself of then
a repressed
anger
frustration
fear
a repressed
tear
a single blood drenched
heart breaking
mind crushing
spirit numbing
faith devouring
self rejecting
image breaking
pain inflicting
soul dividing
life dejecting
death inviting
black depressing
tear

feeling
so forgotten
cry, cry
cleanse it all away
slash drip
die,die
tomorrow will she remember
a scar so sad
they call me Blue

a mystical
deep
rich
fucked
ripped
purified
blue

softly
cold
softly
holding death in hands
felt it slip
like she could feel every grain
like sugar
like rain
through bleeding hands

and in the midst of it all she forgot...

a girl's strife

don't judge me
tattooed spirit and glossy eyes
pierced skin and deep sighs
short hair but still a girl

broken past made me be
the toughest grrrl in the world
strong with steel toe boots and spikes
with words that offend

listen to my spirit not despise
and if I hate macho bullshit
don't call me feminist
call me civilized

tries to tell me how to look and what to say
and tells me to sit down and obey
and be the perfect damsel in distress
but i choose to digress

identity crisis crazy
ridicule of society
you are humanity of hypocrisy
why don't you stop labeling me?

my life is politically incorrect
sorry for the inconvenience
and upon meeting the goddess
who made me i'll whisper thanks

Dearest

daughters of the desert
drowning in despair
dozens disappear
daydreams dissolve
desolate world in denial
dawn breaks to dusk
denouncing death
demanding life
dream on daughters

injustice i see

justice is blind
she has been taken hostage
like the girls from
los ángeles to juárez
she is forgotten
by passersby
sometimes she whispers
i hear her cry

justice is lost
she wants us to find her
like this time
will be different
she is ready
to step up
sometimes she wins
i fear not enough

justice is seeking
she removes her shackles
like the stories from
then and now
she is frozen
in time forever long
sometimes she sings
i hear her song

"we shall overcome
we shall overcome
we shall overcome someday"

injustice i see
unjust life
just once
give us this one

if we fight hard enough
we cannot fail
that our hearts may believe
truth and love prevail

LOVE
amor

Chamber II

All I'm saying

earth babies
spiritual beings
a banner across your chest
underneath heart beating
like there is nothing to lose
only things to gain
like prayers, mantras, & dance
give peace a chance

Eons of light

I remember you
echoes of ancient wisdom
whisper thru me at night
eyes closed heart open
visions of rainbow tribes
hieroglyphics in the sky
rooted deep in Mother Tierra
I've been here before
traveled eons of light
just to reach you

Wanderer

wanderer starstruck lover
seeker of words
keeper of dreams
slowly falling into the wind
amongst trees
catch a glimpse
of all past, present, & future
within the horizon of the sea & sky
forever resilient we fly
dangling from the edge
of el sol
dancing in oblivion
to step of illustrious magik
seeping through my soul
she stole his heart
in one second of intoxicated bliss
revolving around eternal kiss
if i close my eyes
a vision of astounding quest
the planets begin to converse
moments between here & there
tumbling through cracks of wonder
intergalactic space traveler

Oh, my warrior

suspended in space
rainbow warrior walking
across the universe
this verse is for you
i feed you honey elixir
ripened by life
soaked in tears
purified by fire
i quench your thirst
with cherry kissed water
that springs
from my womb
i have been waiting
in dreams i called to you
searched for you outside
far too long
now i know you were
always there
it was me a few steps
behind
i was scared
of this truth
a part of me
being so clever
would run
ahead
so my timing was off
& yet inevitable
cycles aligning
as i sit in silence
close my eyes
open my sight
oh, rainbow warrior
you have traveled with me
forever

Epic Story of a Teen

So so innocent in your eyes
Like the day we-
Shiver and shake open your eyes
Eyelashes curl in a way that embraces touch

True sleek thoughts
Slip through my mind of you
Bubblegum slushies, red hair, orange shirt
So gorgeous delicious

The air feels thick and dreamlike
For the past two days
And I laugh inside

Spiky hair, high water pants cut
To the perfection
Of the non-perfectionist

So so fucked
When the days drift so fast
We grow up unclean
Amidst the drugs and rock n roll scene

Like the time-
We got high
And I cry
I cried for you
So that sadness would become me
And never touch your smile

"You make me smile," he said

Trip hop in the speakers
Streaks of punk rock fire days

"Remember when I loved you?" she said

If it hurts to be in love or
out of love I don't know

Who decides when we grow?
When you know I know more than we should
And the gum wrapper you gave me
Means the world is not numb

girls who fly with crows

when i was younger
someone once told me
& my coven of three
"you girls brought the crows
to the neighborhood"
i didn't know then
what i know now
crow medicine in me
like being two places at once
riding the moon
& hiding the sun
the crow & i are one
he sings to me
flies over me
descends unto me
i tune into him
run under him
lift up to him
there is an unspoken connection
each a reflection
he helps me to fly
& i ground him
black is my favorite color
& he wears it so elegantly
there is untapped magic
between he & i
when i am questioning
he answers
when he aches to be heard
i listen
black feathers
that reflect my spirits flight
we are entwined
like old friends
since childhood & past lives

because i am one of the
"you girls brought the crows
to the neighborhood"
& for that i am grateful

I dreAM

dreamweaving
spiderweb
spiral of life
questions
keep rising
always surface
inside my skin
waiting
wallowing
whispering

dreamscaping
fractals of light
escaping
like sweat
tears &
longing
through my pores
creating
crimson
corazón

dreamcatcher
my yearning
sighs
mixed with
stars
because
i remember
feathers
feeling
forever

dreamkeeper
lucid

memories
reveal
depths
like floating oceans
amidst dimensions
nearing
never-neverland
nomad

no papers, Rosa, no fear

había una vez una Rosa
who got on the bus
an act so small like this endeavor
can change people's lives forever
let us get on the bus
to share the story of us
we are taking a ride
there is nothing to hide
this is our destiny
to cross borders & be free
you see we are some of many
sons & daughters of journey
this road we travel
has been walked on well
many before us fell
we are here to remember & tell
these truths we will yell
beyond fear there is freedom
before papers human hearts come
our time is here
we will not disappear
we will only grow
till our corazones overflow
ancestors by our side
we take pride
our right to be
open your eyes & see
we did not choose this
fate chose us
Undocubus
carry hope, faith, courage, & trust
transporting dreams is a must
four elements
all testaments
if you listen long enough

the whispers of families are rough
we hear them when we sleep
the wounds run deep
the hills we climb are steep
step by step, stop by stop
we will reach the top

there waiting for us is a Rosa
red bursting blood & poderosa
like love that runs through our veins
release rivers of pain
only to build beautiful memories
bring forth communities
a coming together of families
dig roots, plant trees, & let leaves roam
all earth is our home
there is a breeze
it pushes us forward with ease
it gives us aliento
no tiene miedo el viento
había una vez un Rosa
who got on the bus
just like us
carry forth warriors guerreros
de consciencia y voz
somos what dreams are made of
we are sueños of love
creating songs of libertad
toda la verdad
exposed for the world no races
photos of beaming faces
essence of humanity
here is our dignity
no papers, no fear
no papers, no fear
no papers, Rosa, no fear

Palabras Por MI Pueblo

Pienso en tí
cuando sale el sol

Primero tu valor
al dejar tu tierra

Puentes que cruzaste
en busca de algo mejor

Primaveras del ayer
en bellas memorias

Porque tu sueño
era más grande

Preguntas de los que
quedaron atrás

Promesas en el viento
se olvidaron

Préstame tus manos
llenas de sudor

Perdon hacia los que
condenan tú historia

Papel Picado recuerda
ha los que no llegaron

Paredes que se derumban
al soñar

Palomas que vuelan
hacia otro amanecer

Posesión de tu camino
y tu destino

Poder en conocer
otros como tú

Paisanos de la misma tierra
juntos atraves de distancias

Peregrinación es la vida
buscando la razón

Pasajero de la humanidad
no estás sólo

Presente MI Pueblo
por siempre

Tapestry for Tonantzin

Fibers of being
multicolored & entwined
from cosmic stars
& red clay
Your presence my Lady
is all I need to alleviate
my sorrows
my joy I offer to you
via roses & sage perfume
I lay open at your embrace
I retrace my heart
back to your womb
Oh, Tonantzin
blessed Mother
earthkeeper & conveyer
of suplicas
alter these candles
into a light path
that our journey be full
of illuminations
I cling to your mantle of stars
for it reminds me of a home
a universe away from here
I travel the rays of your crown
back to source
for the love of humanity
throw myself at your altar
for the love of my people
uncover temples & cantos
that evoke your enchantment
You are the ultra feminine
La más hardcore, divina, & amada
I unravel this tapestry at your feet
to you mi Virgen
with all my corazón

Sage for the Silent Ones

prayers choked silent like tears

lift up like sage smoke seeking light

let it drift to dark corners

where children hide from bombs

let it carry angels who died too soon

to a beautiful place away from here

let the scent of burning sage

erase the moment of pain

let the fire consume us

for we are them

let this offering ignite

in humans their heart

let us remember the deep

hurt like oceans red

let this cycle be undone

for it has condemned us

let the sage invoke

blessings for silent ones

let it rise to the heavens

like eagles soaring

let the embers solicit

amends for mankind

that will never come

because

the innocent ones

the forgotten ones

the silent ones

will never again

shine their light upon this world

moon rituals for fallen sisters

New Moon rituals that connect cycles
across generations of mujeres

the woman is crying
cry, woman, cry
red tears vision blurring
lamenting one more moon
she left too soon

the mother is fighting
fight, mother, fight
precious flower hits the floor
pain & sadness consume
no witnesses in the room

Waxing Moon rituals build bonds
linking one female to another

the daughter is dreaming
dream, daughter, dream
no more hurting
stars fall upon eyelids
as spirit leaves this world

Full Moon rituals share stories
of healing with the Goddess

the sister is flying
fly, sister, fly
hearts breaking
another fallen feather
we weep together

the woman is remembering
remember, woman, remember

underneath the earth
scars leave traces
of beautiful faces

Waning Moon rituals release rage
rising up of divine feminine

In loving memory of Bree'Anna Guzman & Michelle Lozano.

WE

we are made of clay
one day we will return
from conception to tomb
madre tierra father sky
all things in between
teach us how to fly

we are made of clay
one day we will remember
from the air to the trees
beyond space and galaxies
to live to see to grow
to love to be to know

we are made of clay
one day we will return
from the rain to the ember
bella luna flaming sun
mind, body, soul
three to make us one

we are made of clay
one day we will remember
from beginning to end
amidst lovers and friends
to die to hurt to feel
to cry to breathe to heal

we are made of clay
one day we will return
one day we will remember

Red Leather Heart
for my mamá

My fondest memory of her
standing in red leather knee length boots
they came to represent
her heart on fire
for each one of us
she had a certain look
and we were 5
the fiercest mujer
I've ever known
who loved him
like no one ever could
not even himself
when things changed fast
she held even faster to prayer
she had known this pain before
when leaving her country
plagued by war
she left a piece of her corazón
in the river of her mother &
her father's mountain
she followed her destiny north
like many have done before
she stands here still
weaving our lives with love
& warming our bellies with masa
her tears transformed into agua ardiente
that runs in my veins
I get all my goodness from her
my strong roots &
the dreaming of better days to come

Sacred Dream

We signed up for a mission
A vision to create
El Cielo en la Tierra
Heaven on Earth

Despierta mujer bella
Veniste a vivir sueño sagrado
Sueña despierta
Al amanecer yo ví verdad
En tús alas vuela la esperanza del mañana
Creo ser guerrera espiritual
Viajando entre velos del tiempo
Recuerdo que la humanidad está perdida
La justicia está durmiendo
Abre puertas del espacio
Un manto de estrellas es tu lienzo
Un pensamiento extiende tu luz
Cree en tus sueños
Son los dueños de un nuevo día

Wake up woman of beauty
You came to live a sacred dream
Dream awake
At dawn I saw truth
In your wings flies the hope of tomorrow
I am spiritual warrioress
Traveling through veils of time
Remembering humanity is lost
Justice is now sleeping
Open doorways in space
Cloak of stars is your canvas
Thought expands your light
Believe in your dreams
So it seems will awake to a new day
Awakening moments dream reality into being

Sigue soñando
Thoughts become things become wings
Sueña despierta
We will create a new world
Sueño sagrado

Adelita

mujer de valor y corazón de fuego
en tus ojos brilla la esperanza de la batalla
el mundo no gira igual sin tí
porque tú amor cambia el alma del hombre
mujer de passión y lágrimas de oro
pido tú aura me proteja de mis enemigos
quiero derramar flores sobre tí y no sangre
respirar vida en tu vientre y no guerra
sueño en tu rebozo
que me des calór cuando haga frío
que tú suspiro se trague mi dolor
espero verte en el amanecer de la victoria
un abrazo en el ferrocarril
y el beso que se robo el bandido

Pancho

Soldadera

There's been others
there is only you
A Soldadera
through and through

A Soldadera lives and breathes for you
She fights and dies for you
like a runaway train
marches in the rain
and a stolen kiss under fire

The Revolución would not live on without her
because her love has filled the hearts of men
forgiven pain
and birthed generations of warriors

A Soldadera carries hope and change for you
She laughs and cries for you
like the flare of a gun
protests under burning sun
and a hidden caress under cover

The Tierra would not spin the same without her
because her spirit has penetrated the souls of men
healed wounds
and given us visions of peace again

A Soldadera
through and through
There's been others
there is only you

this is not a love poem

pretty words will not flow forth
from warrior lips
instead all uncomfortable truth
will surface like daffodils
a poison from society
disguised in rose perfume
the rage distilled
from her tears
he will silence ferocious petals
too many times
ignore her raw axiom
love is expected
from the XX chromosome
somewhere this fails
to make sense to her
she carries bullets
like amulets
to defend against
lovely requests
submitting & yearning for boys
will not make the world
a better place
pretty words will not flow forth
from warrior lips

REVOLUTION
revolución

Chamber III

Disclaimer

contents for social change
enclosed within
dare to open
ready to ascend
yes let us rise
avert the crisis
engage the fire
inside your heart
there is no box
this is a spiral
a geometric
perfect flower
blooming
ask why?
see through lies
i see through you
because you are me
we are lovers who
build movements thru
moments of truth
if the sky is blue
paint it red
if the machine is broken
change the thread
do not be afraid
be courageous
break out of the cage
step onto the stage
this is your story
live it with passion
dream it with vision
everything is only temporary
anything is a possibility
welcome to the revolution
we've been waiting

And all the World was in Crutches

Contradiction conduces a thought
in which desolate multitude disappears
Years go by, ideals die
And where do we go?
Down to México - I see
I see a future
for you and me
Between trees & stories of courage

Despite controversy
Defy the constant motion
Give emotion to change
And rearrange
The way we live
or deserve to
Shout and it subsides
Daylight falls unto night

Speak of freedom, liberty
A society, where dreams aren't free
Hunger, loss, pain
Consumer drain
Superior gain
Makes me feel like puking
Rebuking
Standards of law and order

For chaos exists in vain
If not as the source of cosmic existence
Feel the distance
Betwixt the struggle
only to reclaim the fight
Despite labels
We must unite!

Remember It Now

propaganda
mass delusion
gives you visions of fear
wears you down
down the abyss
intoxicated paranoia
you have been lied to

senseless words
static noise
disguised ideals
frequency misused
feeling marginalized
misunderstood
alienated
divided they conquer

our choice is clear
expose
decompose
compost patterns of the past
not meant to last
agenda of the ages
disengages
third eye shut down
open it now

sages must rise up
upward and onward
wave wands of truth
ground self in Earth
build movements
that shake away
tear down
deconstruct

all that is programmed
reset button now

know this
you are heaven sent
brilliant being
of stardust
holding cosmic truths

let it flow forth
before structures and order
chaos came first
perfect explosion of life
descends onto this
dimension outside
space time continuum

gather warriors of the rainbow
together
unite
connect essence
through energetic
cords of light
lift all to higher good

a vast experiment
experience
consciousness
look within to travel far
inside is what you seek
a code that decodes
natural detector of lies
solar plexus
guides your path

global nexus
interlacing ideas
free us

be yourself
question reality
invent your own
create a better world
then recreate it again

always growing
weaver of dreams
believe no one
love everyone
your soul on fire
heart embers
remember it now

And We See

Because there is always more than this
A search for ideals without pain
Identity without a crucified name

And we speak of human dignity
We who are not truly free
While our children take a look and see
We who struggle amidst day & night
Once the finger points to blame
Within corruption & our rights
Where are they now?
As they make us bow
To their political institution
Artificial pollution

And we seek
Seek a truth to keep ourselves sane
More to this than we let ourselves see
Something reminding of the rain
Chaos delivers change
Something about the glamour & glitter
Hidden behind crystalized eyes
Thus despise becomes part of the chain
As we break a cycle
To relieve some of the pain

Look and you shall find
The thoughts that bind together time, rewind
Duality intertwines the mind, body & soul

when

when falling into unrest
do not submit
look up, reach out, & scream
like lightning
under rain
know you're worth more than
you could ever imagine
when descending into madness
do not resist
fly beyond, ignite suspicions, & dance
like wind
under trees
know your essence is more than
you could ever imagine

Resist

Believe you are meant to be
Be where you are meant
No lament No regret
Cascading layers of dissent
Speak you heart don't forget
Shout your truth
Whisper wisdom with your breath
Underneath the stars & moon
I forsee a movement soon
Blissful kiss removes violent fist
A beautiful moment to resist!

This is your Wake Up Call

This is your wake up call
Caracol sounding in the distance
fills the air with vibrations
that shift things
like your mood & perception
your inhale & exhale
because this is not a rehearsal
this is life
This is your wake up call
This is your wake up call
This is your wake up call
Drums beating on the horizon
engaging your senses
on every single atomic level
like your cells & thought patterns
your comings & goings
because there is more to this
this is vida
This is your wake up call

Darkest before the Dawn

It is always darkest before the dawn
it has been dark for so long
i have been sleeping
eyes wide open
then an illuminated path
marked by pyramids &
the descending of the feathered serpent

it is always darkest before the dawn
it has been dark for so long
i have been dreaming
heartbreaking
then a spark of fire
mistaken for the sun &
the rising of my inner light

it is always darkest before the dawn
it has been dark for so long
i have been awakening
third eye blooming
then a flash of sight
musings of new visions &
the returning of rainbow warriors

it is always darkest before the dawn
it has been dark for so long
i have been remembering
soul bursting
then a flaming candle
memories of ancestors &
wisdom keepers returning

it is always darkest before the dawn
it has been dark for so long
i have been consumed

spirit transforming
then an exploding galaxy
mixing me with the milky way &
the coming of spring

Are you Listening?

Actions speak
louder than words
silence holds the space
louder than bombs

I see you marching
thru mountains of green
I hear you even
when you say nothing

For we are one in the same
we are revolutionaries of heart
spanning the web of stars
our corazón carrying grace
no need to see our face

Pasamontañas reveal the eyes
only the windows to our souls
emerge fierce & lit with fire
the doors closed long before
only bridges beginning to surface

Winds of change
shift the leaves of our
ancestral trees
stand strong like ancient temples
of remembrance

The capitalist plague
will not take hold of our roots
because together we move
like rushing water
swiftly cleansing
scarlet stains & death
in our path

Stillness speaks
silence thunders
we peak like rainclouds
embracing the sun
we make ourselves heard
by telepathic knowing
a sixth sense that is growing

Do not fear the roar of Giants
for they are few & their time is gone
listen to the whisper of the Cosmic Earth Keeper
for they are many & their time is here

This is not *Just* Poetry

This is not *just* poetry
it is visions pouring
thru us of collective
conscious unity

These words flow
thru us catching glimpses
of a new world aglow
revolutionary

The love we speak
is a reflection of
the truth we seek
in humanity

This is not *just* poetry
it is justice screaming
thru us in constant
vowels & soliloquy

The musings on this page
a distilling forth
thru us of rage
transformed as poetry

The ideas we write
come forth streaming
no wrong or right
only questions on being

This is not *just* poetry
it is life revealing itself
thru spoken word
this is the sound of urgency

There are those whose verse
some would silence
so we grow louder & disburse
create freedom of speech treaties

The stitching of phrases
as declarations of change
us only leaving traces
messages as visionaries

This is not *just* poetry
it is equality pleading
thru us in pain
requesting mercy

These odes emerge
thru us hearts beating
as we converge
under skies so starry

The rhymes it seems
count us into
the daydreams
of our journey

This is not *just* poetry
it is every moment
of overlooked pieces
unknown & mystery

The ink begins spilling
a memento of silence
thru us of feeling
becoming a story

The voices in our head
come from living
in black & white then red

adding color to memory

This is not *just* poetry
it is death beckoning us
thru dark nights
this is the typist bleeding

There are those whose lyric
some would ban
so we sing louder & euphoric
never sorry no apologies

The poets manifesto design
of grasping fleeting thoughts
turning letters into lines
free even if charged with just poetry

* Dedicated to Qatari Poet Mohamed Ibn Al Ajami
sentenced to life in prison for reciting a poem.

Smiles, Feelings, & Presidents

there is a feeling
that seeps into me
when watching politicians
smile that knowing look
the we have fooled them
again kind of grin
I stopped following
these events long ago
& I haven't been around
very long it seems
when I was born
Jimmy Carter was one
of those sneering men
& Barack Obama was writing
poetry at Occidental College
just blocks from where
I lived in 1979
he didn't know he would become
The President
& I didn't know I would become
The Poet
the smirk had not yet found
its way to his lips
the deception of politics
evades young Dreamers
until too many times
believing that smile
I realize they are all
the same united under
one new world order
the hope dangled
like the blazing sun
blinds the people
into thinking all is well
in AMERICA

people go to work
or unemployment
people go home
or into foreclosure
people go to sleep
or stay awake thinking
about the smile
of privileged greedy men
who make this nation
go round & round
the merry capitalist go around
& I get this feeling
so I look away
to a better place
the face of skies above
connecting
constellations of change
so I will become the mother
who worked twenty years
as an activist
so her daughters
could stand there
smiles transformed
by feminine wisdom
& collectively lead
una AMERICA unida
a united AMERICA
where eagles & condors & quetzals
fly together under
one transparent sun
& the feeling becomes love

To be a Pocha or not to be

because I'm neither
from here or there
I speak both languages
with a flair
born in Los Angeles
with roots that extend
reaching out to faraway lands
faraway sands, faraway from here

because I'm my father's daughter
drowning in alcohol
seeking the metaphysical
calling back in time
my family line
a forgotten leaf
on the familia's tree
to be a Pocha or not to be

because I'm my mother's daughter
drowning in depression
seeking a connection
recovering memories
of a tierra I never knew
a forgotten trace
of ancestors in me
to be a Pocha or not to be

because I'm not good enough
for here or there
i love to hate my flag &
hate to love my creation
ashamed of spanish in the 1st grade
i'm sorry mami i never meant to hurt you
ashamed of english in abuela's embrace
i know you never meant to hurt me

because I'm merging culturas
every time I breathe
crossing borders
every time I speak
split forever into one
at the edge of two worlds
the edge of possibility
to be a Pocha or not to be

because I'm finding a balance
of this cosmic raza
a fusion of color
for this mestiza
things to learn
and things to teach
the little ones in front of me
to be a Pocha or not to be

meet me @ noon

my soul hits the asphalt at noon
adorned with multicolored textiles
transported into the jungle
bubblegum sidewalks
lead me to pyramids
pretend skyscrapers are trees
the rhythm of this life
brings me to my knees
there is more to this
i do confess
meet me at noon
we will transverse
this mess
a deep breath
takes us somewhere far
where you can sees stars
no more cares
only here do i see
you are me
a connection so deep
it traces back in time
reminds us
we are wildflowers
not followers
but autonomous beings
whose roots break asphalt
always, everywhere
especially at noon

Dream Act

Dream Act
like waiting to come home
become known and seen
because I have a story...
I live and breathe like you do.
I sleep and dream like you do.

Dream Act
like a thousand voices
carried in the wind
telling stories and asking...
Why deny me your ideals of liberty?
Why ignore me after you claim equality?

Dream Act
like a nightmare
where I can't wake up
struggling for rights
a piece of paper &
your stamp of approval

Dream Act
a dream deferred
american dream is dead
falling under lies
under broken promises
under votes

Dream Act
like an ancient memory
humanity is the same
we all bleed and laugh
and most of all
we will continue to DREAM...

Malinche

Sometimes someone comes along
that tries to change the beat of the drum
This is change & it is different
This is new & non complacent
There are few who will embrace it
Most will reject it
Some will suspect
All will affect it

There is this thing engrained in our cultura
the confusion that stems from 500 years of ruptura
instead of uplifting each other we drag each other down
with words, silence, energy & being too guera or too brown
something unseen deep in our roots
if someone rises we shoot
a dis-ease with our own gente
the cure is in our mente

The color of privilege has nothing on the color of hate
lines are blurred we forget we ache
ignore the cries we extract from each other
forget i'm your sister you're my brother
nos olvidamos que somos humanos
global humans cosmic beings
remember we are reflections of ancestors
if i hate myself i hate you
if i love you i love myself

Malinche sangre runs in the veins
slash it away & release the pain
out of our experience comes a new sun
the luna lights our new dawn
the wounds we heal
build trust & begin to feel
I will embrace her & spit her out

because the cosmic raza has no room for betrayal
there is only us & we are royal
descended from temples of jade & turquesa
a mix of pura belleza

Sometimes someone comes along
that tries to change the beat of the drum
let us begin to listen
to reconcile we dance
in a harmonized trance
for we must lend each other a hand
this is our madre tierra & land
embrace it & each other
we will rise together

CONNECT THE DOTS...

This is how solidarity grows
connecting dots on the map
till the boundaries overflow
painting flowers on the walls

Building bridges as a whole
helping neighbors keep control
keeping it local
less is more

If stories repeat themselves
which they do
learn from the bad
take from the good

Como Chavez Ravine
& Wyvernwood
No 710 El Sereno
& destroying our hoods

I see a pattern building
of taking land
then rebuilding
let's take a stand

Started long long ago
over sacred community
must end the light show
interest groups under scrutiny

Gentrification
is a virus killing
spreading silently
essence of us drifting

Across time and space
connect the dots on the globe
brings us to this present place
oppressors dominate

Remember ancestors vividly
witness the unfair
environmental racism
current state of affairs

If stories repeat themselves
which they do
denounce mistakes
reclaim our truth

Like people gathering
creating conscious art
open space like gardens
& centers with heart

I see roots rising
despite loud noise & laying cement
cutting down hearts of green
life doesn't need your improvement

Strumming music in the streets
let's dance together
advocate alternatives
only for the better

Generations converge
our hearth not for sale
never was, never will be
so take your leave we will prevail

Fueling Feminine Fires

You are either born a feminist or become one

dedicated to my daughters & son

You either fight repression

or become part of the problem

You stand up for womyn's issues

& work to solve them

You give voice to your Sisters

& learn to love them

You stop explotation

& start to empower femme

You question patriarchy

& create feminine stems

You reject mysogeny

or unconsciously flame it

You give up stereotypes

& claim natural beauty

You uplift the female

every time you embrace her

You came from a mujer

& this is a blessing

You respect yourself

& the rest will follow

You remember your divine

& the goddess is everyone

You are a feminist or become one

& raise fist in the air for generations to come

rEVOLution = noituLOVEr

you say you want a revolution
been running in my head for awhile
came to a conclusion

it's not about bombs & guns
it's about hearts & songs
cause we're headed for a new sun

too much talk not enough action
ideals once claimed
get caught up in distraction

building bridges that connect
envision change
no one suspects

keep up resistance
connect the dots
across the distance

one by one
hold together our world
things are coming undone

the system will burn
the moment is now
it is our turn

you say you want a revolution
been running in my head for awhile
i wanted one too

EVOLUTION
evolución

Chamber IV

occupy yourself

the system is sick
these words are our medicine
shedding my skin
like the new sun
that is rising
calling my ancestors in for some guidance
cutting away all the cords of violence
like the calm before the storm
there is silence

give me sight
that i might see
beyond the lies
surrounding me
that i may let go
of what i don't need
because i've been falling
falling
falling
free falling
in lives both past and present
thru cycles of material lament
ideas planted inside of me
like weeds destroying
the greed is growing
the forest dying
the wind is crying
the volcano exploding
the ocean rising
it is rising
we are rising
ride the current
activate your essence
plant the seeds of resistance
watch them grow in the distance

brothers & sisters across the planet
this time will be different

occupy your life
least they take it
like adjust the bill of rights
afraid of our flight
they try to cut our wings
seduce us with things
translucent mind games
give you more of the same
inducing the youth
poisoning our fruit
with their chem trails
domesticating our children
with the abc's & the 123's
forgetting that which they came here to be
warriors of light
warriors of insight
warriors of rainbows
they wanted you to fail
alchemy transforms this reality
another way to engage
when enraged
is to meditate
there is humanity at stake
the seers at the lake
foretold this tale
try to wake you from slumber
the hundredth monkey awake
reveals the system is all take & more take
forgotten to breathe
losing air
hope is fleeting now...
remember to breathe
fists in air
love is being in the now...
occupy yourself

it begins from within
that thing that you're seeking
has always been
movements come & they go
you resist & you flow
like clouds drifting
remind me that
revolutions give way to
evolutions give way to
love
like the chants you let out
to let the healing in
the visions you carry
into daylight from dreams
it is more than this
it is this & more
occupy yourself
& you will know
watch it grow
emotions overflow
the wind whispers &
trees speak to those who listen
all else has come to pass
the future calls us back
star travelers
story tellers
let me tell you a story
of how things came to be
you see there was a shepherd
a shepherd herding the sheep
only this shepherd was also asleep
tell me where your dreams went
time for mass dissent
on every continent
question all content
ask again & again
until the answer comes from within
a divine connection

all the children know
the adults will not listen
they do not know how
programmed without realizing it
hypnotized with television
tell me where your visions went
you fallen star
traveled far
descended from heavens & dimensions unknown
unknown here
I know where that place exists
deep within your interior
a light
burning truths
let it expand let it grow
there are seeds to spread & sprout & sow
like love: a key to unlock the doors
a window is open now
gives a glimpse of the soul
the soul the spirit the thing
you know the thing which gives you life
gives you wings
gives you things unseen & opens more
creation is a symphony
elevate humanity
is this bliss I've come upon
the 99 percent is waking up &
we are strong
burning the myth created
the phoenix rises
from the ashes
letting my ancestors in with guidance

occupy yourself
choose love & life will survive
this system is sick
& these words are our medicine
like the calm before the storm
there is silence

It's a beautiful day

to unplug from the matrix
go outside
stand barefoot in the grass
look up at the clouds
hug a tree
breathe in breathe out
& believe in dreams

Seeking

mortal flight
blue bird sipping on water
looking for a way back home
fell upon a black hole
drifting thru galaxies
from a time before
i miss my star so
magenta is my favorite color
swirls of feelings came before
we danced together for a moment
then i slipped back thru the window

Bliss

A BLESSING IS THIS
EARTH OF PYRAMIDS i KISS
LABYRINTH OF JAGUARS WHERE EAGLES FLY
SOUL MERGES WITH THE SKY
ANCESTOR SPIRITS BREATH OF FIRE UPON ME
WHISPER ECHOES OF ANCIENT MEMORY
WHERE THE SUN & THE MOON MEET AS ONE
i COME UNDONE

i

search self for stories to be told

behold the voice comes alive on this page

this whole world a stage

each to play their parts

guide yourself with your heart

navigate the labyrinth of stars

look within to go far

be aware of every moment

do not lament

every encounter is a choice

use your voice

learn to listen & speak

in the silence lies what you seek

4, 3, 2, 1

unified under the elements
fire, water, air, & earth
our home & our hearth
eons of time
which do not exist
calendar ticking
2012
a new awakening
bind us on to
the stage set before us
a play in two parts
of devil's advocates & idealists

Looking Infinitely For Eternity

life is this
melancholy
confusing
longing
enthralling
soul searching
spirit crying
fingertip touching
maze
a maze
a journey
your life in slow motion
your life in slow fucking motion
with the music in your head
the music
the beat
the rhyme and reason
drumbeat becomes your heartbeat
the soundtrack
the complete musical background creates
it creates
the life you had
the life you have
the life you hope for
it creates
the mood
the gloom & tear
the joy & laughter
the echo of your soul
the repetition
repetition
repetition of the echo
your spirit
fingertip touching
spirit crying

soul searching
enthralling
longing
confusing
melancholy
this is life

Emerge

Time is accelerating
The spiral spinning faster
Urgency-Emerge-ncy
Begin to spread truths
Listen to others
Take action
Observe
The arts of believing
Manifesting
Positive thinking
Conscious dreaming
El presente
Is already here
Parallel lives merging
The matrix is about to implode
The stars foretold
The cosmos unfold
Open your eyes
Open yourself beyond space & time
Open your mind

7 generations

we were here first
we will not be the last
we are the next 7 generations

shades of earth
children of the sun
descended from stars
in sync with the moon
hearts like drums
hands of gold
eyes like obsidian
keepers of medicine
4 elements
4 directions
foretold
prophecies unfold
cosmic race
a sea of faces
the eagle and the condor
return to balance

we were here first
we will not be the last
we are the next 7 generations

Spirals

Deep within the core that subdues the restlessness
Find the essence which will make sense
Leave all pretense behind
Dwelling in the abyss of ultimate creations
There is the truth waiting to be told
Behold the voice of eternity
Transformed by what will be
There is this
This is now
Now is here
Here we are
Are we real
Real it seems
The dream continues
Rolling on & on
Search in & inner still
Till thy find
The limits of the mind
None
One is all
All are dreaming
Start awakening
Begin believing
Crescent luna
Burning Sun
Long to know the stars of time
Time dissolves
There is no end
The cycle is beginning
Always mending
To live
To give to self
To love
To rebirth
Nurture the virtue

The veil unfolds
The gift is present
The knowledge gold

Bird Tribes

return of the feather tribes
remembering past lives

uncover your wings
every plume under skin

you've been a bird before
or an angel in mid flight

you've been flying thru ages
seeking life to engage in

return of the feather tribes
choose to come again

dust off your panache
take in infinite sight

decipher your dreams
listening to signs

inked this spirit on skin
awake dna codes from within

return of the feather tribes
you are here
have always been
alway will be
remember you have wings
& you can fly

Rising from the Ashes

I AM the Phoenix burning
& it hurts every cell of my being
transformation isn't easy
changing is very messy
feels like ripping in two
seeping through you
I'm on the edge
jumped off the ledge
catapulting towards concrete
at a very fast speed
you see I asked the universe
to guide me
deep spirit & soul searching plea
but it's not all butterflies & rainbows
it's deep & dark & full of shadows
purify the pain with fire
before it gets easy it gets harder
it gets intense before it gets lighter
we are at a crossroads
each one chooses their own
yet all lead to ONE
people of the SUN
it is time to RISE
the ashes left behind
we take flight
we take might
we make it right!

Night Tripper

the mystic train has left
the station where i lost
stardust clouds &
the glitter of my eye
my sighs were heard
on monday morning
reaching the echo
of an empty space
inside a soul's caress
a mess of candle wax
dripping onto the floor
the door wide open
asking for change
same station
parallel tracks
the creation of subways
thru the subconscious
spirits rushing by
intoxicated fumes
enhanced by dark lights
deep shadows &
under stairwells
the elevator to heaven
is out of order
the next ride is not until
seven
on the tracks
sleeping off
the last five lives
forgotten
the cost of admission
because i have wings

the lighthouse

a guidepost
along
the way

the daybreaks
as my heart
shatters

window pains
inside
this house

a light
turned on
at midnight

to calm
the stormy waters
of me

shh

there are pieces
shattered
mirror glass
still
holding a reflection
of me
the moment of impact
came so fast
I hesitated
only after
it was over
having looked at myself
within myself
around myself
so many times
it was boundless
to break
the narcissist self
spills
onto everything
I touch
but how do I remove
myself from me
wouldn't that feel like dying?
wouldn't it?
the letting go of familiar
gasping for air
my heart closing
its doors & valves
the window to my soul
stuck
my eyes no longer
reflecting light
the color
seeping

from my cheeks
my ego fighting
until the bittersweet end
for a little chance at the
spotlight
not knowing
we are always center
stage
each & everyone of us
every moment
every breath
you cannot outrun
your destination
you must not give up
nor give in ever
you must lift the pieces
create a mosaic
of new memory
for the sun is rising
in the east again
someone
else will wake
take some
steps
into the unknown
eyes wide open
heart beating
search
for the mirror
that will reflect truth

the return of the writer

the flow makes things lighter
no lament
every experience
a test of your essence
a taste of bittersweet
the balance of duality meets
each a scar
left to remember near or far
be who you are
raise the bar
each a story to reflect
every death leads to resurrect
the journey is full
good or bad equals beautiful
make the best of this
turn ache into bliss
take the lesson
everything happens for a reason
create music out of pain
then dance in the rain
the versus will flip
all life is a trip
keep seeking your truth
inside of you
a spiral leads us within
follow the sound to begin
sleep lets us awaken
dark leads to light
black to white
night to day
silence to say
tears to laughter
before to after
closed to open
& i like you

will be here
to see things thru
take it all in let it out
listen up write it down
down deep
then my soul
can dream of new wonders
wonderful new ways of being

and so it is

i am ready to manifest
are you?
you are here now
so am i
together we entwine
rise up like kundalini
like vines
seeking the sun
knowing the light
is the way back to one
stemming from this place
outside space
dreams are reality
anything you can envision
you can be
this is the time
to release your inhibitions
to believe your intuitions
risk yourself in everything you do
be yourself beyond anything be true
healers, visionaries, dreamers
come forth & rise
realize you are wise
within seeds of beautiful sight
plant them deep
slowly they creep
up the asphalt of doom
green sprouts make room
catch air & fly
reach out to the sky
so high
that they may take root
in the stars
in the galaxy they ignite & reach far

no limits only yes
this is only a test
check check 1 2 1 2
use your voice
like the microphone
share all you've known
bare your soul
lose control
reach for impossible
teach miracles
create vehicles of change
the rules rearrange
think outside the box
create ripples of shock
color outside the lines
be on the lookout for signs
coming forth from above
become love
because that is all that we are
agents sent from the stars
messengers of all relations
rainbow vibrations
frequencies of thought
the speed of light
what you think you become
think bright & glow
when you grow I grow
in sync we flow
if you shine i rhyme
if i cry you sigh
let's build the bridges
no more ridges only flowers
engage your powers
bring them forth
believe your worth
the words become songs
taking flight

into uncharted territory
a new story
let there be light
and so it is

Corazón

today I awoke with Fire

burning through my heart

speaking universal tongue

my spirit bursting like stars

a strong felt desire

to rise up and manifest

feeling ready for revolt

and I ask you

where did you leave your Corazón?

falling under and over the rise of the moon

someone left too soon

& you forgot to close the door

what is in store for you now

what will you reach for soon

an eclipse and setting sun

tell me when did you forget that we are all one

who invaded your divinity?

gave you false ideals & comprised liberty

tell you how to dress

how to feel

what to choose

what you can afford to lose

the reality is you were born free

daughters & sons of the galaxy

be bold in your search for truth and equality

where has humanity left their Corazón?

sowing seeds of discontent

reinvent the self

and I could only hope

the system is broken & destined to fail

it consumed you

and here we go again

inner sigh, intuitive eye

a dream unseen

chaos & creation

invented this space inside of you

to keep the secret of a people

remember it now

you must rise above

cleanse again

like feelings & rain

create beauty to reflect

believe in truth & love

and most of all awaken

to your Corazón

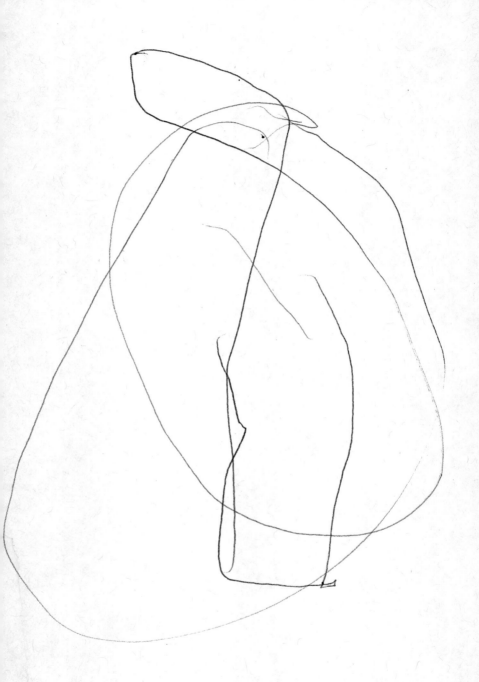

124

Acknowledgements

Behind every good person is an even greater community. I AM blessed and humbled to have a strong foundation around me. It was an act of courage on my end to leap forth and self publish this book but it would not have been possible without the support of many people.

First of all to my family and friends, who have believed in me every step of the way. My patient esposo, Jovan Frias, and my blooming seeds: Xion, Isis, & Ixchel who allowed me to immerse myself in the making of this book. To my brothers, George, Jesse, and James who inspire me with their lives to keep growing. To my sister, Lynda, for being my rock and believing in dreams just as much as I do. To my mom, Adelina, who showed me to always follow my heart and have faith. To my dad, Jose, for teaching me the value of hard work and imagination. To my partners in crime, Christina Cervantes and Katia Valenzuela, thank you girls for reminding me of my roots and that together we can fly.

I extend my deepest gratitude to my cousin, Paul Alejandro Herrera, for designing the cover. To my cousin, Haide Gamboa, for her skills in photography. To Brent E. Beltrán for your advise and craft. To Alfonso Aceves and Adriana Carranza (Kalli Arte) for the collaboration on the artwork and bringing my ideas to life. To Robert Loza (Sol Soul Designs) for developing my website. Once again to Lynda De Anda for being my second pair of eyes and knowing my idiosyncrasies well enough to leave certain words as is.

Then there is my community of beautiful people. So many to list, but a special recognition to everyone at the Eastside Cafe in El Sereno who have given me a space to call home where I can develop ideas and help create the world I want for the generations to come. To everyone at the Healing Arts Center of Altadena for allowing me to grow my gifts in the healing arts and teaching me to ground my visions into action. To all the strong mujeres that surround and inspire me. The power of the people is a beautiful thing to witness.

Last but not least, everyone in my poetry community including Poets Responding to SB1070, who realize the need to use our words as a catalyst for change. To La Bloga, for providing a platform for this Pochita. To all the poets I've ever had the privilege of sharing words with; your passion and dedication to the art of writing have given me hope. Words are our medicine.

About the Author

Iris De Anda is a writer, activist, and practitioner of the healing arts. She is a woman of Mexican & Salvadoran descent. A native of Los Angeles, she believes in the power of spoken word, poetry, storytelling, and dreams. She has been writing for most of her life and this is her ceremony, her offering, and her creation for a better world.

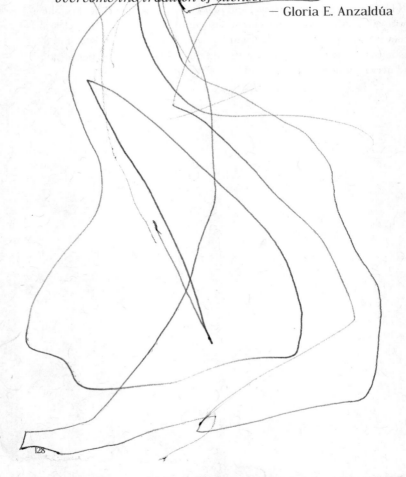

"Until I am free to write bilingually and to switch codes without having always to translate, while I still have to speak English or Spanish when I would rather speak Spanglish, and as long as I have to accommodate the English speakers rather than having them accommodate me, my tongue will be illegitimate. I will no longer be made to feel ashamed of existing. I will have my voice: Indian, Spanish, white. I will have my serpent's tongue – my woman's voice, my sexual voice, my poet's voice. I will overcome the tradition of silence."

— Gloria E. Anzaldúa